CARVER
POLICY GOVERNANCE®
GUIDE

T0307729

ENDS
and the
OWNERSHIP

Revised and Updated

JOHN CARVER
MIRIAM CARVER

JOSSEY-BASS
A Wiley Imprint
www.josseybass.com

Published by Jossey-Bass
A Wiley Imprint
989 Market Street, San Francisco, CA 94103-1741   www.josseybass.com

Library of Congress Cataloging-in-Publication Data

Carver, John.
   Ends and the ownership: a Carver policy governance guide / John Carver and Miriam Carver.
—Rev. and updated ed.
      p. cm. —(The Carver policy governance guide series)
   ISBN 978-0-470-39253-9 (alk. paper)
   1. Corporate governance. 2. Boards of directors. I. Carver, Miriam Mayhew. II. Title.
   HD2745.C37224 2009
   658.4'01—dc22

                                                                    2009003149

Printed in the United States of America
REVISED AND UPDATED EDITION
HB Printing   SKY10082110_081624

The Carver Policy Governance Guide Series

The Policy Governance Model and the Role of the Board Member
A Carver Policy Governance Guide, Revised and Updated

Ends and the Ownership
A Carver Policy Governance Guide, Revised and Updated

The Governance of Financial Management
A Carver Policy Governance Guide, Revised and Updated

Adjacent Leadership Roles: CGO and CEO
A Carver Policy Governance Guide, Revised and Updated

Evaluating CEO and Board Performance
A Carver Policy Governance Guide, Revised and Updated

Implementing Policy Governance and Staying on Track
A Carver Policy Governance Guide, Revised and Updated

Praise for the Policy Governance Model

"Reading these guides is a great way to start your journey towards excellence in governance. All the essentials are there, short but clear. And these six guides will also prove to be an excellent GPS device along the way."

—Jan Maas, PG consultant, Harmelen, The Netherlands

"The guides are a great way to introduce busy board members to the basic principles of Policy Governance. Their bite-size approach is inviting, covering the entire model, albeit in less detail, without overwhelming the reader. They are succinct and easy to read, including practical points of application for board members. Consultants asked to recommend initial reading about the model can do no better than these guides."

—Jannice Moore, president, The Governance Coach™, Calgary, Canada

"Boards introduced to Policy Governance quickly become hungry for information but are short on time. These guides help board members quickly absorb the key principles of the Policy Governance model. They are invaluable."

—Sandy Brinsdon, governance consultant, Christchurch, New Zealand

"For some board leaders the governance elephant is best eaten one bite at a time. The Carver Policy Governance Guide series provides a well-seasoned morsel of understanding in a portion that is easily digested."

—Phil Graybeal, Ed.D., Graybeal and Associates, LLC, Greer, South Carolina

"Would you or your board benefit from a quick overview of essential governance concepts from the world's foremost experts on the topic, John and Miriam Carver? Thanks to their new six-booklet series, you can quickly familiarize or refresh yourself with the principles that make Policy Governance the most effective system of governance in existence. These booklets are the perfect solution for board members who are pressed for time but are dedicated to enhancing their own governance skills."

—Dr. Brian L. Carpenter, CEO, National Charter Schools Institute, United States

All organizations exist on someone's behalf. We don't mean the persons they exist to benefit, though it is possible for these to be the same people. A large group, such as a community, could decide to have an organization that benefits a small group, such as people without literacy skills. Or a small group, such as members of a particular church, could decide to have an organization to benefit a large group, such as impoverished people in developing countries. In these instances, the community and the church membership are akin to shareholders, that is, owners of the respective organizations. The boards are stewards on behalf of the community and the church membership. And in fulfilling that trust or stewardship, the board clarifies whose lives shall be benefited or changed, and which part of the life experience of a targeted population will be different than it might otherwise have been. And since resources are always limited, the board expects the operating organization to yield enough of that result to be worth what the effort costs.

We all know these things; they aren't new insights. And yet we are all also accustomed to organizations, particularly nonprofit and governmental organizations, being somewhat unclear or even confused about who, for them, are equivalent to shareholders and, for them, what the difference in beneficiaries' lives should be. This is odd, since surely the only way we can tell if an organization is even worth existing is by ascertaining if, in light of owners' values, it makes enough of the right difference for the right people to justify its cost.

By contrast, many organizations are very clear about what they *do*, that is, about what keeps the staff busy. For many organizations, it appears that being busy at commendable activity is the test of organizational worth, and being effective is disregarded. Yet we must know that being busy is not the same as being effective at making the right difference for the right people at the right cost or priority. How odd that we confound being busy with being effective. And how odd that sometimes, in an activity-focused world, simply being busy comes to be treated as if it is, in fact, a result! So having a new program up and running for the planned expense, processing a number of clients through the clinic per dollar, or having so many children in a swimming class for the expected per-child cost are treated as effectiveness. Programs and activities that can demonstrate cost-busyness are treated as if they have demonstrated cost-effectiveness. Distinguishing between what an organization is for and what it does is a basic feature of the Policy Governance model. This feature is the ends-means distinction.

In this Guide, we begin by explaining ends and give examples of Ends policies. (We will capitalize Ends when referring to a board's actual Ends policy documents but not when referring to the idea or concept of ends.) Development of Ends policies is driven by the other topic of this Guide, the related issue of ownership, for it is on the owners' behalf that the board makes ends decisions. So we will go on to explain the ownership concept and explore some of the options a board may use to connect with its organization's ownership. We will argue that more than any of the decisions that a board must make, decisions about what the organization is for should be made with owners' values in mind.

But first, we will provide a brief overview of Policy Governance in case you have not read it before or need a reminder. If you understand Policy Governance well, you can skip this section of the Guide.

Policy Governance in a Nutshell

- The board exists to act as the informed voice and agent of the owners, whether they are owners in a legal or moral sense. All owners are stakeholders but not all stakeholders are owners, only those whose position in relation to an organization is equivalent to the position of shareholders in a for-profit corporation.

- The board is accountable to owners that the organization is successful. As such, it is not advisory to staff but an active link in the chain of command. All authority in the staff organization and in components of the board flows from the board.

- The authority of the board is held and used as a body. The board speaks with one voice in that instructions are expressed by the board as a whole. Individual board members have no authority to instruct staff.

- The board defines in writing its expectations about the intended effects to be produced, the intended recipients of those effects, and the intended worth (cost-benefit or priority) of the effects. These are *Ends policies*. All decisions made about effects, recipients, and worth are *ends* decisions. All decisions about issues that do not fit the definition of ends are *means* decisions. Hence in Policy Governance, means are simply not ends.

- The board defines in writing the job results, practices, delegation style, and discipline that make up its own job. These are board means decisions, categorized as *Governance Process policies* and *Board-Management Delegation policies*.

- The board defines in writing its expectations about the means of the operational organization. However, rather than prescribing board-chosen means—which would enable the CEO to escape accountability for attaining ends—these policies define limits on operational means, thereby placing boundaries on the authority granted to the CEO. In effect, the board describes those means that would be unacceptable even if they were to work. These are *Executive Limitations policies*.

- The board decides its policies in each category first at the broadest, most inclusive level. It further defines each policy in descending levels of detail until reaching the level of detail at which it is willing to accept any reasonable interpretation by the applicable delegatee of its words thus far. Ends, Executive Limitations, Governance Process, and Board-Management Delegation policies are exhaustive in that they establish control over the entire organization, both board and staff. They replace, at the board level, more traditional documents such as mission statements, strategic plans, and budgets.

- The identification of any delegatee must be unambiguous as to authority and responsibility. No subparts of the board, such as committees or officers, can be given jobs that interfere with, duplicate, or obscure the job given to the CEO.

- More detailed decisions about ends and operational means are delegated to the CEO if there is one. If there is no CEO, the board must delegate to two or more delegatees, avoiding overlapping expectations or causing disclarity about the authority of the various managers. In the case of board means, delegation is to the CGO unless part of the delegation is explicitly directed elsewhere, for example, to a committee. The delegatee has the right to use any reasonable interpretation of the applicable board policies.

- The board must monitor organizational performance against previously stated Ends policies and Executive Limitations policies. Monitoring is only for the purpose of discovering if the organization achieved a reasonable interpretation of these board policies. The board must therefore judge the CEO's interpretation, rationale for its reasonableness, and the data demonstrating the accomplishment of the interpretation. The ongoing monitoring of the board's Ends and Executive Limitations policies constitutes the CEO's performance evaluation.

Ends at the Beginning

The Policy Governance view of decisions is that in any organization, though there are uncountable numbers of decisions being made, causing all sorts of circumstances and conditions, there is a class of decisions that can usefully be separated from all the rest. This class, which we call ends, includes all decisions about the differences, results, or outcomes to be created by the organization in the lives of intended beneficiaries; all decisions that identify for which beneficiaries those differences are made (the beneficiaries are external to the organization, not the staff or the board); and all decisions that designate the cost-effectiveness or priority of the difference made (we use the word *worth* to address both these types of cost). We often use a shorthand way of stating these three components of ends: "What difference, for whom, at what worth?"

Why is it necessary in Policy Governance to separate ends issues from all others? The answer is simple. Ends issues describe the purpose of the organization in cost-benefit-beneficiary terms, while all other issues, as important as they may be, do not. This three-part ends concept is as powerful and essential as it is simple. Let's examine the three components of the ends concept in more detail.

Difference   This is a matter of effectiveness. To express the difference an organization exists to make, there are a number of words that would work. Sometimes *result* is a better word. Or for some organizations, *outcome*, *impact*, or *change* is more useful. But at root, what we are talking about here is the difference made in people's lives. Someone may get a monetary return on investment. Someone who could not previously read now can. Someone with no place to live now has a home. Someone had a serious illness and recovered or now knows how to be independent despite the illness. The population of a region has sufficient fresh water. The general public has an understanding of the dangers of smoking. These are changes—or differences made—not in the organization but in the lives of the people the organization seeks to affect.

Beneficiaries   This is a matter of targeting. There are persons the organization exists to benefit, so the changes made must be for these people. Organizations that seek to have an impact in the world but fail to clarify who should feel the impact risk the misdirection of effort and the production of unnecessary impacts with their attendant costs. The words normally used for beneficiaries vary with different types of organizations. In a general sense, words like *recipient, target population, client,* or *consumer* can work, but they can also be confusing. For example, while for a nonprofit organization *beneficiary* and *consumer* might mean the same thing and can therefore be used interchangeably, in an equity corporation, *consumer* means a person with whom the company hopes to make profitable transactions. In that case, consumer is not the same as *beneficiary*, since the persons for whose benefit the corporation exists are shareholders. A further caution is that a given person might be in more than one class. For example, the beneficiaries cannot be board members or staff in their roles as board members and staff. Since it is possible for a member of staff to also be a beneficiary in the way that a corporate employee can own shares or a health clinic provider can also be a patient, it is important to keep the roles or "hats" people are wearing straight.

Worth   This is a matter of efficiency or priority. This third component of ends deals with the worth of the right change for the right recipient. At the broadest level, the meaning of worth is that the results produced must be worth what they cost. If it is possible to produce literacy skills in adults for \$X, producing these skills for \$X + 1 suggests that the organization is not as efficient as it should be. We use the term *worth* because it can cover two instances of cost-benefit: first, the straightforward cost of results in terms of money, and second, the cost of results in terms of other results forgone. The latter expression means the same as *priority*, one result against another. When organizations produce several different results for several different recipient groups, the worth of results can always be expressed in both ways and the board may wish to control it in both ways.

The three ends components incorporate effectiveness and efficiency into one concept. They can be visualized in a simple input-output diagram like Figure 1.

Figure 1. The Black Box with Its Inputs and Outputs.

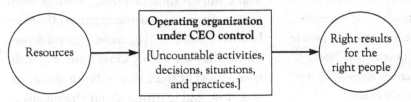

In Figure 1, we show the operating organization as a black box. We are not sure what's going on in it, but we know what goes into it and, if we make some hard choices, what we want to come out of it. We know the organization is a consumer of resources, including money but in many cases unpaid volunteer resources as well. We know that the organization has outputs, and we know they should be the right outputs in terms of changes or results for the right people. Requiring that there be a favorable relationship between input and output is the greatest fiduciary responsibility a board has, even though when fiduciary responsibility is discussed by most boards, it is typically about far less important variables. The board's chief accountability is that the organization it governs produces enough of the right changes for enough of the right people to justify the resources consumed. It is that cost-benefit-beneficiary complex that comprises the Policy Governance ends concept. It is our observation that even organizations that have long lists of goals and objectives and procedures usually still do not have board-stated ends.

You can see from Figure 1 that the activities of the organization are not ends issues. Using the definition we introduced in the Carver Policy Governance Guide *The Policy Governance Model and the Role of the Board Member*, non-ends in Policy Governance are called means. Therefore, all aspects of an organization except for the ends elements are means; some are operational means, some are board means. (Board means include only those necessary for the board to accomplish its outputs, the "values added" we describe in detail in the Carver Policy Governance Guide titled *Implementing Policy Governance and Staying on Track*.) Despite the predominant importance of ends, obvious even from a diagram, it is incongruous that the boards of many, maybe most, organizations, unless they are Policy Governance boards, spend most of their time talking about, inspecting, and learning about the means of the operating organization. It is a remarkable feature of traditional governance that ends are rarely discussed beyond occasional reference to the beneficiary component. But even if a board has clarified who the beneficiaries should be, this clarification is usually in terms of the relationship of persons to a staff activity or service rather than to a result in their lives.

> So if you are a board member, it is extremely important that you not use *ends* and *means* in the way we all do outside of governance. Treat them as code words, not normal speech.

Distinguishing Between Means and Ends

In nonprofit and governmental organizations, we have noticed a strong tendency of boards to refer to services, programs, projects, or curricula as if these were ends. Of course, they are not ends. While one can hope they produce ends, in themselves they are just activities conducted by staff. However, it is impossible to tell if they produce the desired ends if the ends to be produced have not been defined and separated out from all the possible ends that might have been chosen. Even closely examining programs, services, curricula, and projects cannot reveal if the right ends are being produced or even if any ends are being produced at all. Examining means can only expose if means are being conducted; whether or not they work remains unknown.

To illustrate further: job skills are the kind of result that qualifies as ends, while job training is means. Adequate shelter qualifies as the result component of ends, while a homeless shelter program is means. Ample water supply in the African Sahel is an ends issue, while well development is means. A market return on shareholder investment is an ends issue, while manufacturing automobiles is means. Because ends describe the organization's purpose in terms of outcomes, recipients, and worth, their accomplishment justifies the existence of the organization. Nothing else does. It is for this reason that being able to tell the difference between ends and means is a crucial skill for Policy Governance board members.

> So if you are a board member, try describing your organization without mentioning its activities, methods, staff, or organizational design. If you cannot, then notice that your understanding of the organization is not about its effects in the world but its types of busyness.

Over the years, we have observed that some board members find the ends-means distinction confusing and that some boards waste valuable time in disagreements about whether a matter is an ends issue or not. We have always found that boards in this position have made the ends-means distinction much harder than it really is. We should admit that the choice of the words *ends* and *means* to describe these two concepts may have contributed to the problem, for in general parlance these words are used to carry a number of meanings. The Policy Governance usage is not the dictionary definition. The words are merely code words for two Policy Governance concepts, necessary because their precise definitions are not communicated by any other terms in use. For example, *goals*, *objectives*, *strategies*, *tactics*, and *procedures* do not carry the needed meaning and would import problematic baggage.

There is little difficulty in maintaining the distinction if a board simply asks itself these questions about any given issue: Does this decision describe the desired results in recipients' lives? Does this decision describe the recipients whose lives are to be changed? Does this decision describe the worth of the desired results for recipients either as measured against resources or against other results or recipients? Unless the answer is yes, the issue must be one of means. If the answer is yes, it is one of ends. Ends issues are about one or all of the three elements: results, recipients, and worth, and nothing else. Most of the confusion we've seen occurs because a board fails to follow that simple rule.

When we find boards confused about the ends-means distinction, we find that the stark simplicity of the distinction as just stated has been confounded with additional, irrelevant factors. We have heard board members say, "It must be an ends issue because it's important." But the ends-means distinction does not separate issues based on their importance: ends are certainly important, but so are means. We sometimes hear, "It must be an ends issue because the board should decide it." But the ends-means distinction does not separate issues based on who should decide them. In fact, the board makes policies that control ends and it also makes policies that control means, while staff make ends decisions and operational means decisions as well. Other sorts of confusion we have encountered include "It's ends because it's about money," "It's means because it is about cost," "It's ends because it's legally required," "It's ends because the board should have a policy about it," "It's ends because the board is accountable for it," "It's ends because it describes a time for completion," "It's means because it is a smaller part of a decision already made," "It's ends because it affects the result," and on and on. All of these examples ignore the only definition that applies in Policy Governance: it's ends because it designates the required result for beneficiaries, the identification of the beneficiaries, or the worth of those results. And means are means for no reason other than they are not ends.

It makes a difference that the board gets this right. In fact, Policy Governance will not work unless it does. As we have noted, means allowed to masquerade as ends in board Ends policies ensure that the board is requiring the organization to be busy rather than to be effective and efficient. In addition, the Policy Governance board sets prescriptive policies to control ends but prohibitive policies to control operational means, so being able to tell ends and means apart is an essential step in crafting policies consistent with Policy Governance theory.

Developing Ends Policies

Consistent with the mixing-bowl principle, Ends policies are written with a long-term perspective first at their broadest level, then further defined by the board until the board is satisfied that it can accept any reasonable interpretation. At that point, the policy is delegated to the CEO, whose obligation to further define them yields more detailed ends.

For organizations incorporated under for-profit statutes, the ends issues are mainly or in many cases exclusively centered on return on owners' investment. The difference to be made can commonly be expressed in financial terms, and the intended recipient is the shareholder. (You may have noticed that the shareholder is both owner and beneficiary.) After all, when people open businesses, they open them to make money. They may open them for other reasons too, of course; perhaps you know people who in addition to wanting to make a living in their own business also value the experience of being their own boss. When for-profit businesses grow, and particularly when they seek capital, the primary purpose for the business is that investors get an acceptable return on their investments.

> So if you are a board member, cultivate the habit of "seeing through" activities to the results they are ostensibly intended to yield. This will help you avoid being bedazzled by impressive or interesting activity.

In market-driven organizations such as these, it may be relatively simple to define organizational purpose, since the return that will tempt an investor to invest in your business must be competitive. The capital market is a major and useful reference point in determining

> So if you are a board member, you will have the chance to learn about the trends that suggest the likely future needs that the organization should meet. You will have the opportunity—indeed, the duty—to meet with those who can assist you and the board in learning about and deciding on the direction of the organization. You may well find ends deliberation to be the richest discussions your board has ever had.

what the return to owners should be. That doesn't mean a corporate board has no ends work to do. The board may require a lower than average return on investment for a short while if it believes that this would make a more competitive return possible in the long run. Further, because there are several ways to express shareholder value, the board must think strategically about which definition is most likely to cause a satisfactory performance in future markets as they seem to be evolving.

In the case of organizations incorporated under not-for-profit statutes and for governmental organizations such as libraries, counseling agencies, municipal governments, and mental health authorities, deciding on ends is much harder. Such organizations operate in a muted market or in some cases in no market at all. What constitutes a doable yet challenging level of effectiveness and efficiency must be decided by deliberation rather than by the automatic workings of a market. In effect, the board is a market surrogate, deciding what it is worth to produce what for whom. It is for this reason that most of the examples of Ends policies we will be giving in this Guide will be ends for nonprofit and governmental organizations.

But before we embark on a series of examples, we will list a number of tips and points to remember when formulating Ends policies. Following these tips will help your board to write policies that really are about ends.

1. Expect this to be challenging. Boards often think that they have already been clear about ends or that Ends policies are quite self-evident. But rarely is this the case. In the

situation of limited resources, a reality for most organizations, deciding who will get what is inextricably tied to deciding who will not get what. The values decisions involved in Ends policymaking are difficult and very high-leverage.

2. Your current mission statement and strategic plan are unlikely to be written in ends terminology. If they are, congratulations. If they are not, it will be interesting to notice that the board has heretofore required activity, not results.

3. As a board sets out to decide its broadest Ends policy, remember that the job is not to produce a slogan or a motto. Public relations value is not the aim here. If a slogan is needed for public relations reasons, it can best be established by the CEO, consistent, of course, with board policies.

4. Ends policies, while they should be ambitious and long-term in perspective, have to be actually possible. They are not meant to be idealistic in the sense that they cannot be accomplished, yet they are your board's most exciting opportunity to be bold. Remember that the board's Ends policies form a large part of the CEO's job description. If your Ends policy requires the CEO to produce "a world that works for everyone," good luck filling the job.

5. Ends policies must describe what it is the CEO's job to accomplish, not the board's philosophy, theology, or worldview. Your board's philosophy, theology, or worldview are important and may be a major reason that people volunteer to serve on the board, but they describe the board, not the board's expectations of organizational effectiveness and efficiency. If your board wishes to make a statement in its policies about its own beliefs, couch this statement as a Governance Process policy.

6. When the board is deliberating about ends in preparation for deciding what ends to require, it should put aside all

concerns about how to measure them. This may sound
strange, but you will remember that board policies are made
measurable by the CEO's interpretation of them. There is
no need to worry about how the CEO will measure your
policies if you have defined them to the "any reasonable
interpretation" level. Measurement is a hard thing to do,
but it's not your hard thing to do. If you try to make policies
measurable yourself, not only is there a risk that you will
sacrifice what is meaningful to you in the service of measur-
ability, but by doing so, the board will have plunged into a
much more detailed level than otherwise it would have
chosen. For example, for a given school board, "literacy at
grade level" might be sufficiently detailed (any reasonable
interpretation of literacy and grade level is acceptable), but
"a score by more than 90 percent of students greater than
the 60th percentile on the Johnson Reading Examination,
as nationally normed" not only narrows the definition of
the board's expectation but requires considerable board
study to be sure this is a reasonable measure of the broader
statement (which the CEO otherwise would have to prove).

7. Further definitions (lower levels) of ends must be ends.
When the board has written the broadest policy and is
unwilling to accept any reasonable interpretation from the
CEO of that policy, it needs to further define the policy.
That is, the next level of policy narrows the CEO's available range of interpretation of the larger policy, so it must
observe an identical ends discipline. Narrowing ends, in
other words, doesn't take them into means.

8. All sentences contain verbs, but watch out for them. If the
organization is the subject of the sentence and the verb
"belongs" to it, you can be sure you have written a policy
about means. If the intended beneficiaries are the subject
of the sentence and the verb belongs to them, it is much

more likely that the policy is about ends. Compare "We teach reading" with "Children can read." The first prescribes an organizational activity, which apparently need not work just as long as it takes place. The second requires a designated outcome for a designated group. Monitoring "We teach reading" results in the board's receiving evidence that teaching has taken place. Monitoring "Children can read" results in the board's receiving evidence that learning has taken place.

9. In particular, look out for "effort words," as these are imbued with so much righteousness that they may tend to get a free pass. Policies requiring advocacy, support, and quality services are about means. Policy wording that the organization will contribute to, help with, or pursue ends does not require the achievement of ends, only the attempt to achieve them.

10. Be careful about words such as opportunity and access. They may be results, but they really lack ambition. A community college board requiring that people have "the opportunity to learn" this or that is not requiring that they actually do learn this or that. A parks board requiring that people "have access to enjoyable recreation" is not requiring that anyone actually avail themselves of the access. Is the party worth its cost if no one comes?

11. Beware of words that are ambiguous in that they could describe an outcome but also could describe a process. Education is such a word. A policy stating that "children be educated" could mean either that kids have a certain level of knowledge or that they are being taught. Therefore, even a correct ends intention risks a misinterpretation as the process of educating, a means. It is better to avoid ambiguity by describing what the children should know or be able to do.

12. Be sure that the ends your board writes are the ends of your organization, not someone else's. For example, trade associations do not produce the ends that their members produce. The association of mental health centers does not produce mentally healthy people, though it is to be hoped that its members do. Associations produce something else. What?

13. The first and broadest Ends policy should be broad enough to contain all other ends expectations, and this policy should include all three ends elements: results, recipients, and worth. Subsequent Ends policies can omit one of the elements, but the board must be aware that omitting worth or priority, for example, delegates to the CEO the authority to make the decisions about worth and priority. Likewise, failing to further define the consumers or the results signals that these decisions are delegated to the authority of the CEO.

14. Maintain a good understanding of why it is important to get this right. This is not mere wordsmithing. A board that previously demanded a day care program (a means) could require ends such as "Working parents have peace of mind about the safety of their children," but it could alternatively require that "Preschoolers acquire school readiness skills." These two ends are very different and would require different means to accomplish them. Notice how organizational characteristics required for one would be different from those required for the other. They would differ in terms of the cost of production, hours of operation, qualifications of staff, needed equipment, and other elements of production (all means).

15. Moving from the global, broadest level of Ends policy to the second level can result in several further definitions at the second level. But if you find that you have moved from the broadest level to the listing of many further

definitions, consider the possibility that you have skipped a level, thereby plunging into more detail than is necessary, at least at this time. As if an intervening "bowl" has been skipped, go back and decide a more general second level.

Examples of Ends Policies

In the examples of Ends policies shown as Exhibits 1 through 6 in this Guide, you will see that the wording can differ somewhat. Some boards like to express their Ends policies in the present tense, while others choose to use the future tense. This is a matter of preference and makes no difference to the utility of the policies. Optionally, the board can choose to state the time at which accomplishment is expected. You will see in the examples that the board may choose to describe the priorities it assigns to its further definitions of ends. This is a valid but optional choice. Some boards decide that to exercise this choice is unnecessary, thereby automatically granting the CEO any reasonable interpretation of the priorities.

By the examples shown, we are not suggesting these specific depths into which a board should go with its Ends policies. These examples would make our point if they were briefer or if they were longer, for the proper depth is determined when a specific board goes as far and no further than the level at which it can accept any reasonable interpretation.

Exhibit 1. Example Ends Policy of a Trade Association.

The association of Floor Tilers exists so that there will be conditions conducive to member success, sufficient to justify expenditures comprising dues comparable to similar trade associations and reasonable user fees.

In order of priority:

1. Members have business skills.

   a. Members with long-term business experience will acquire the ability to use up-to-date technology.

      b. Members new to the business will understand the legal and regulatory requirements they must meet as business owners.

2. There is strong consumer demand for floor tilers.

      a. Consumers prefer tile over carpet.

3. There is a forum for member networking and exchange of information.

Exhibit 2. Example Ends Policy of a Public School System.

The purpose of Smartville Public Schools is that, sufficient to justify the expenditure of available revenues, young people of the district will have the knowledge and capabilities they need for successful transition to the next stage of their lives.

1. Numeracy and literacy skills at grade level.

      a. Literacy in two languages, one being English, for students who have superior learning capacity.

2. Knowledge of the major historical and geographical features of the world.

      a. A thorough understanding of the history and geography of our country.

3. The ability to search for and find information in a self-directed manner.

4. An understanding of science and technology sufficient to function in the modern world.

5. Where chosen, an understanding of subject areas sufficient to allow admission to appropriate further or higher education institutions.

6. Skills for entry-level employment.

7. An understanding of the diverse world in which we live and a knowledge of the demands of good citizenship.

Exhibit 3. Example Ends Policy of a Mental Health System.

The Relax County mental health system exists so that people with mental health, developmental, and substance abuse challenges live as independently and productively as possible in an understanding county, worth the expenditure of available funds.

1. The first priority is that those with acute illness will rapidly resume optimal functioning.

    a. Persons susceptible to acute episodes of illness will know how to prevent these episodes and how to respond to their occurrence.

2. The second priority is that people with chronic illness will have a productive and enjoyable way to spend their time.

    a. Those capable of work will have jobs suitable to their health status.

    b. Those disabled by their condition will enjoy acceptance and friendship in as independent an environment as they choose.

3. The third priority is that persons with addictive disorders, including to alcohol and chemicals but excluding gambling and chocolate, will control their addictions and live lives minimally impeded by them.

    a. Those at risk of developing addictions will be aware of the dangers they expose themselves to and have the ability to choose more healthful behaviors.

4. The public of Relax County will have knowledge about mental health issues sufficient to moderate stereotypes and minimize stigmatization.

5. Family members of any patients will have the information they need to be as understanding and as helpful as they choose to be.

Exhibit 4. Example Ends Policy of a Credit Union.

Members of the Bricklayers' Credit Union will optimize and control their financial lives.

1. Members have up-to-date information about their finances and can deposit, withdraw, and transfer funds on a 24/7 basis.
2. Members with suitable credit histories will have credit on competitive terms.
   a. Personal but not commercial mortgages.
   b. College loans.
3. Depositors will receive a competitive yield.
   a. Minor children of members will experience the benefits of saving.
4. Members will have the information they need to make wise financial plans.
   a. Members approaching retirement will have the ability to make decisions about wills, trusts, and distributions from retirement savings.

Exhibit 5. Example Ends Policy of a City Council.

The city of Fairtown is a pleasant place in which to live and work, worth the taxes paid.

1. Citizens and visitors, no matter what their personal economic situation, can travel around and through the city with ease.
   a. Pedestrians can negotiate the city safely.
2. The city, public streets, and buildings are clean and in good repair.
   a. No accumulated trash or snow.
   b. No abandoned vehicles or potholes.
   c. No sewage accumulation or contamination.

3. There is a diversified economic base that supports the natural environment.
4. Citizens and visitors can access cultural resources, open space, and recreational options.
5. Economically disadvantaged citizens can find housing, medical attention, and temporary financial assistance.
6. Citizens, visitors, and businesses are safe from crime, fire, and other common hazards.
7. Neighborhoods and subdivisions of the city are livable communities.

Exhibit 6. Example Ends Policy of a Listed Equity Corporation.

The ultimate aim of the company is exceptional return on shareholder equity greater than the return for firms of similar risk characteristics.

1. Risk characteristics for comparison will include similar size, industry, and maturity of market.
2. Exceptional return will mean above the median for such firms, but in no event less than a rolling three-year average of 12 percent compounded growth in annual earnings per share.

As you can imagine, the board's Ends policies are decisions with great leverage. They resolve issues of great moment, ones undoubtedly open to widely and often passionately held opinions. They are almost always subjective on a grand scale. Reasonable people differ about what should be produced, for whom, in what priorities by our organizations. Board members disagree among themselves and should see their strength in their ability to act resolutely despite disagreement. But the spread of opinion among board members expresses only part of the relevant diversity. Because the board represents others, giving voice to the diversity of those on whose behalf the board governs is what matters—a far more daunting task. And to do that well begins with the board's recognition of what, in Policy Governance, is called the ownership.

The Ownership

For closely held companies in which all the owners are on the board, it is quite understandable that the board would make decisions in its own interests. But most organizations are not like that; the board and its members don't own the organization. That's why Policy Governance boards accept that they exist to make decisions on behalf of those who do own it. In effect, then, boards are agents of the ownership, trustees who decide in the best interests of owners. Policy Governance boards know that they are a link in an unbroken chain of command that starts with owners and doesn't end until the most junior staff member on the organization chart.

So who are owners? For some organizations, this question is very easy to answer. Shareholders own equity corporations. Parent companies wholly or partly own subsidiary companies. Members own trade associations, professional societies, labor unions, and credit unions. Citizens own city government, though not in the usual legal sense of property ownership. Those are easy. But who owns community-based nonprofit organizations like some hospitals, counseling agencies, and children's centers? Who owns international relief and development organizations? Who owns the health charity?

Even when there are no legal owners, it is useful to see all organizations as having owners in a moral sense. For that reason, Policy Governance incorporates the concept of moral ownership. The meaning, of course, has nothing to do with morality in its most frequent meaning but rather a bond perhaps more accurately described as virtual ownership, like saying the citizens of a state own the state government.

In Policy Governance, the concept of ownership, whether or not it has legal reality, serves the function of establishing a legitimacy base outside the board. It reduces the chances of the board's behaving as if the governed organization actually belongs to the board, the staff, or present beneficiaries. It gives the board a reference point and a source for input when the board decides on ends. Owners after all have the right to decide the purpose of what is owned or if they cannot do so due to awkwardness of numbers, to be the dominant influence on the board as it makes ends decisions as their agent.

The Policy Governance ownership concept has given some boards considerable pause. Most boards would readily agree that they do not make decisions on their own behalf, but when asked on whose behalf they make them, they are seldom sure. That means that as the board has been making decisions, the unspoken truth is that it has made them on behalf of different and unexamined concepts of its trusteeship. Often the board has not decided the question or even taken it seriously. We have seen attempts to define the board's legitimacy base that are extremely useful, but we've also seen boards jump to seemingly attractive but flawed ownership designations. Here are some examples.

Are the stakeholders the owners?   Stakeholders are persons who have a stake in your organization: the neighbors who hope it doesn't make too much noise, the staff who depend on it for a livelihood, the vendors who sell supplies to it, and on and on. While there is no doubt that an ethical obligation is owed to such stakeholders (the organization shouldn't make too much noise, be unfair to the staff, use purchasing methods that don't give vendors a fair shot at the business, or pay its bills late), this hardly makes them owners. A lot of people have a stake in our personal cars, including those who service them and those we buy gas from. But we own the cars, and no one ever gets that confused. Stakeholders include owners but form a category that is too large to be useful in determining ownership.

Are constituents the owners?   Politicians frequently speak of their constituents. Sometimes they mean the general public or a district of the public from which they were elected, in which case they may have in mind something near or identical to the Policy Governance ownership concept. But sometimes they mean persons who want or receive government services, that is, who are in a customer or beneficiary role rather than an owner role. The problem with the term *constituent*, then, is this ambiguity.

Are the clients or consumers the owners?   Once again, we can easily see that the beneficiaries (in nonprofits often called clients, patients, or students) are people to whom much is owed, but does this make them owners? There are some organizations in which the owners and the beneficiaries are groups that almost totally overlap. Credit unions and mutual insurance companies, for example, are owned by their members, who are also their customers. But ownership and customership are different roles, ones with different characteristics, deserving to be honored in different ways. Credit union members as owners can themselves or through the board acting as their agent clarify what they want the credit union to produce. But credit union members as customers can receive a car loan only if the board acting on behalf of and in the interests of owner-members has decided the credit union is in the business of producing credit for personal vehicles.

There is a logical problem in considering recipients, consumers, clients, or customers to be the owners solely because they are in those roles. On whose behalf was the decision made that they would be beneficiaries? Ownership has to preexist in order for the customer decision (which is an ends decision) to be made on the owner's behalf. Most boards understand that the world changes such that the appropriate beneficiaries for today may not be the most appropriate ones in the future. But if boards make decisions about who the recipients will be on behalf of those who are today's recipients, how difficult would it be to designate other groups as tomorrow's recipients even if shifting needs makes a change the sensible choice? Ends decisions about who will be the beneficiary of what the organization produces are also decisions, by default, about who will not be recipients. It's hard to decide on behalf of present consumers that they will not be future consumers.

Are funders the owners?   Many nonprofit and governmental organizations receive funding from public or private sources. They depend heavily on the funding and are wise to deal with funders with a great deal of respect. They are obliged to comply with the terms of the contract under which funding was granted. But even though they are important, are funders the owners? If funders are offering money for purposes other than those the board intended to be fulfilled, the organization has the choice to refrain from applying for or accepting the money. Indeed, that is its ethical obligation, and to fail in it results in organizations that will accept money from any source and allow the organization's purpose to be whatever funders want. Under these circumstances, it is hard to perceive an urgent need to have a board at all. Funders are organizations with whom organizations enter into a bargain, but they are arguably not owners.

Are donors the owners?   This question is closely related to the previous one but focuses on the individual donor rather than institutional funders. Do donors not make a decision to donate to an organization because they support its purpose? If they do, its purpose must have been decided prior to the donor's donation. On whose behalf was the purpose decision then made? With few exceptions, donors are part of the ownership but not the entirety of it.

Are the employees the owners?   Only in employee-owned corporations. But many nonprofit and governmental boards act as if the staff are the owners. They make the decisions that the staff place in front of them to approve and get almost all their information from them too. For some public boards, such as city councils or school boards, the staff dominate the election process, thereby becoming the de facto ownership instead of the general public. It is easy to see the public policy flaws inherent in staff as ownership. Surely, boards have an ethical obligation to ensure the fair treatment of staff, but that is very different from allowing the staff to assume ownership prerogatives that would make them the superior authority over the board.

Getting to Know the Board's Boss

It can be difficult to settle the question of who the owners are, but it is a question that is worth pursuing. After all, if you own an organization, you have the right, we suppose, to run it into the ground or drive it in the wrong direction. But if you don't own it and are accountable to its owners for the decisions you make, knowing who the owners are seems like a good idea. Knowing who the owners are allows you to ask them what they have in mind for the organization's purpose. We were amused, some time ago, to see a criticism of the Policy Governance ownership concept in a journal. The author criticized the concept on the grounds that ownership is hard to determine and that therefore it is a concept that is not useful. We are relieved that most people don't give up that easily. We can think of many things that are hard but still worth taking pains over. Flying a plane and performing surgery come to mind.

There are some organizations whose ownership is particularly difficult to determine; public radio stations in the United States are a good example. But the ownership concept still has utility in such cases in that it focuses board attention on a rich discussion of those to whom the organization owes its allegiance, whether or not resolved without dissent, and it prevents the unintended bestowing of ownership prerogatives on staff, current beneficiaries, or a founder. Normally, however, the board discussion of ownership engendered by the question resolves the issue in a way both satisfying and constructive.

Physical Communities and Communities of Interest

It has been our experience that many boards of community-based nonprofits regard the community, be it a town or a state or province, as the ownership. The board of a community-based counseling agency, for example, may decide that it is making decisions about ends on behalf of the community as a whole. And it has also been our experience that many other boards find the concept of a community of interest helpful in determining the moral ownership. We have encountered many boards for which this has seemed the right answer. The board of an international relief agency decided that it would be useful to see itself as making ends decisions on behalf of those who are concerned about and committed to ending hunger and sustaining the environment. It is important to note that even as a fiction, this decision allows the board to focus its information gathering antennae on those it has called owners and thereby be able to improve the representative nature of decision making.

Why Ownership Matters

Boards that understand that their decisions are on behalf of identified others easily see the need for consultation with those others. This is not public relations or fundraising. It is not so much an exercise in telling about the organization as it is about listening to input about it. In Policy Governance, the relationship between a board and the ownership is quite as important as the relationship between the board and its CEO. Weak links in the chain of command damage all links below them, as CEOs who struggle with internal delegation when their own link to the board is ambiguous can attest. In some types of organizations, a few outspoken owners can cause a board much pain and difficulty when the board has itself not firmly coupled itself to the ownership as a whole. One need only watch an association board or a publicly elected board be battered by individual owners acting as if they represent all owners simply because owners in general are out of the loop. Governance in general has greatly underplayed this connection between boards and owners. That is what is going on when a corporation treats shareholder relations as an executive function.

> So if you are a board member, your board has a staff schooled in the "how" of management and programming or production but no more qualified to make decisions on behalf of the ownership than you are. Do your job, and let them do theirs.

Connecting with the Ownership

But understanding the important link that should exist between ownership and board does not settle the question of how that linkage can be established, particularly with owners too numerous to sit together for discussion. Deciding how to connect with owners probably needs to begin with debunking the many counterfeits of ownership linkage.

The most common bogus methods are public meetings and public hearings held by publicly visible boards, councils, and commissions. We have found, as you may have already discovered, that waiting for their owners to come to the board with valid input could involve a very long wait. Public boards that hold open meetings are to be lauded for doing the public's business in public, but the people who show up tend in the main to be staff, potential vendors, disgruntled consumers, and reporters hoping to see something controversial.

> So if you are a board member, just listening to numbers of people, even if they truly are owners, is not enough. Board decisions are on behalf of the total ownership, not just those who take time to lobby you.

Take the school board as an example: meetings are open due largely to "sunshine laws" for transparency in conducting the public's business. While open meetings may well address that purpose, they do little for ownership linkage. Some or even most of the people in attendance might also be owners, but it is not their ownership role or attitude that motivated them to attend. And even if they were all there as owners, self-selection makes what they have to say as owners virtually unusable. Yet school boards act as if their meetings constitute connecting with the public. In fact, they are a pretense of including the public, all the worse in that the hollow practice seems to make it unnecessary to pursue real ownership-board linkage.

Large ownerships can only be heard by extreme measures of reaching everyone or by far easier measures ensuring an acceptable statistical probability of representativeness. Inferential sampling of large populations is a mature science that promises boards a high confidence that they know the values of their ownership on relevant matters. Yet few boards use such samples on a regular basis. Policy Governance uncomfortably confronts boards with this shortcoming.

Some boards decide that the community is the ownership from which they get their moral authority and then notice that the community is also the ownership of many other organizations as well. The boards of the counseling agency, the city, the nonprofit hospital, the parks district, and other organizations have the same or greatly overlapping ownerships. Not only that, but their ends, while not necessarily overlapping, when taken together define much of what a community is. Yet they rarely talk with each other. Board-to-board communication as an approximation of board-to-owner linkage is not only more manageable for many boards but a potential opportunity for cost sharing in setting up ownership input systems. It is unfortunate that this, too, happens rarely.

But making sure owners' input is on relevant matters demands that opportunity for ownership input be carefully structured. What are the governance-relevant questions for which a board needs answers? To continue the school board example, to get from the ownership opinions about the best way to teach reading, how to organize school bus routes, or the most customer-friendly way to arrange the school calendar would draw owners into decisions that shouldn't even be made by the board, much less the board's boss. The wisest gathering of owner values would be to help with the momentous ends questions a board faces—in effect, the reasons for having the school system to begin with. Wouldn't it be refreshing for boards to ask, "What technical abilities do you think children will need to have to be successful in twenty years?" or "Is competence in at least two languages worth forfeiting other educational outcomes, and if so, which ones?" Boards approaching the public in meaningful ways not only get the decision information they need but by doing so put the public back into public education. Settling on the right questions is crucial to getting useful owner input.

So boards that want to be responsible agents of the ownership must find a way to affirmatively reach out and include consultations with the whole span of elements of the ownership. Waiting for owners to come to the board always fails and is certain not to inform the board with a fair representation of the diverse viewpoints. In most organizations' ownership is great diversity; ownership linkage is incomplete if that diversity is not respected and sought out.

> So if you are a board member, you are part of a group that is the starting point of organizational authority held on behalf of the owners. If you are a nonprofit board member, you are probably unpaid; by definition, this means you are a volunteer. But don't let the term *volunteer* belittle your role: you are as morally obligated as if you were paid.

For a board to be a responsible agent of the ownership requires, then, a rationally derived identification of owners (unless their identity is obvious due to the nature of the organization), a method for hearing owners' values and opinions that is statistically respectable, and a carefully constructed range of governance-relevant questions for owners' reaction. It is not that a tabulation of owner input, no matter how valid, in itself determines what the board decides, say, about ends. The board must also add to its owners' wishes whatever further knowledge the board may be privy to but that owners cannot be expected to know. The board must also consider what it knows about its organization's capacity in order not to assign undoable expectations. In other words, the board in this scenario is not just an adding machine but a reasoning body that acts with wisdom not gathered solely from owners but that is at all times in owners' interests. This kind of expert agent role is not an uncommon one. In retaining a lawyer, for example, we expect our interests to be served but for the lawyer's special knowledge to be used to do that.

We have in this Guide made the case that the most momentous decisions a board makes are ends decisions and that the closest relationship a board should have is with the ownership. For too long boards have, instead, put most of their influence on operational means and nurtured their closest relationship with staff.

Conclusion

We have argued in this Policy Governance Guide that it is important that a board understand on whose behalf it makes its decisions. This reference group, which we call the ownership, forms the legitimacy base for the use of board authority. Further, we argued that possibly the most important decisions a board should make are ends decisions. Ends decisions, by determining whom the organization should benefit and what the nature and worth of the benefit should be, describe the only real justification for any organization's existence.

About the Authors

John Carver is internationally known as the creator of the breakthrough in board leadership called the Policy Governance model and is the best-selling author of *Boards That Make a Difference* (1990, 1997, 2006). He is co-editor (with his wife, Miriam Carver) of the bimonthly periodical *Board Leadership*, author of over 180 articles published in nine countries, and author or co-author of six books. For over thirty years, he has worked internationally with governing boards, his principal practice being in the United States and Canada. Dr. Carver is an editorial review board member of *Corporate Governance: An International Review*, adjunct professor in the University of Georgia Institute for Nonprofit Organizations, and formerly adjunct professor in York University's Schulich School of Business.

Miriam Carver is a Policy Governance author and consultant. She has authored or co-authored over forty articles on the Policy Governance model and co-authored three books, including *Reinventing Your Board* and *The Board Member's Playbook*. She has worked with the boards of nonprofit, corporate, governmental, and cooperative organizations on four continents. Ms. Carver is the co-editor of the bimonthly periodical *Board Leadership* and, with John Carver, trains consultants in the theory and implementation of Policy Governance in the Policy Governance Academy.

John Carver can be reached at P. O. Box 13007, Atlanta, Georgia 30324-0007. Phone 404-728-9444; email johncarver@carvergover nance.com.

Miriam Carver can be reached at P. O. Box 13849, Atlanta, Georgia 30324-0849. Phone 404-728-0091; email miriamcarver@carver governance.com.

Notes